PICTURE PROMPTS STORY STARTERS

58

Creative Illustrations

for creative kids

© 2024 30 Minute Circle Time

ISBN: 979-8-986467201-14

I0161615

30 MINUTE CIRCLE TIME

Picture Prompts Story Starters

Copyright ©2024 30 Minute Circle Time

All rights reserved. No portion of this book may be reproduced, store in a retrieval system, or transmitted in any form or by any means, electronic, mechanical, photocopy, recording, scanning, or otherwise, without written permission of the publisher.

ISBN 979-8-9864672-1-4

Printed in the USA

www.30MinuteCircleTime.com

Picture Prompts Story Starters

Introduction

Why Use this Resource

Congratulations on your purchase of a valuable classroom tool! This assortment of 58 engaging and detailed illustrations will ignite your students' imagination for creative writing. These illustrations serve as excellent prompts for various writing styles and can enhance any writing curriculum. They can also be utilized as a form of "filler" activity during instances when students find themselves with extra classroom time.

Organization of the Book

Every worksheet contains an image along with a list of words associated with it. A line is provided for the title of the story, and multiple lines are provided for the story itself. The word list consists of keywords related to the picture, which will help the students to begin to think about their overall impression of the image. To spark creative thinking, students are encouraged to read the word list before writing, and they may even incorporate those words into their story if they choose to do so.

© 30 Minute Circle Time

Picture Prompts Story Starters

At the end of this book, you will find a page with blank lines. It serves as an area for students to either draft a story outline or extend their story if they require additional room.

This book includes:
- Steps to writing a great story.
- A list of words to use instead of "said".
- Reminders to use capitals, punctuation, quotations & what to do when unsure of spelling.

Students, how to use this book:
- Find a picture prompt that kicks your imagination into high gear.
- Decide what should happen in your story and how your story will end.
- Start writing!

These engaging story starters include silly animals, funny situations, and other strange and fun subjects that are perfect for elementary school kids and up. Once the story is written, your child can have fun coloring the creative illustrations.

Picture Prompts Story Starters are easy to use and perfect for parents or teachers who want to inspire their kids to write and create.

With our fun story starters, your child will have endless opportunities to explore their creativity and develop their writing skills. They are also a great way to spend quality time together as a family!

Write with heart, creativity, and happiness. Believe in your story and let your imagination fly!

30 Minute Circle Time

These stories belong to

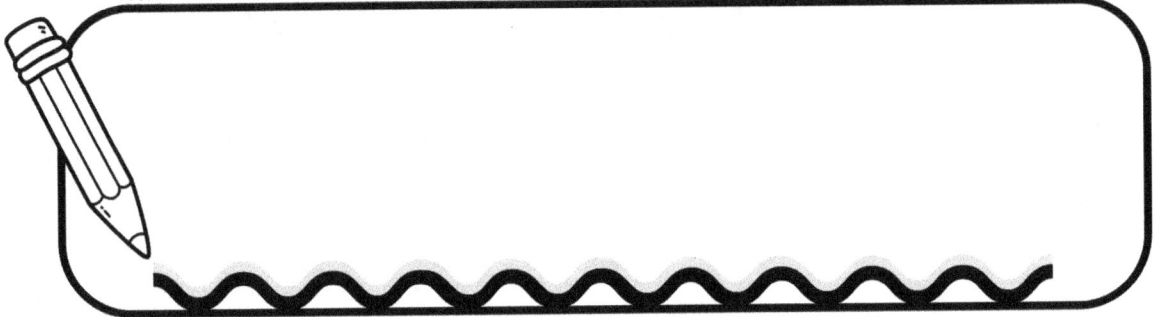

© 30 Minute Circle Time

Punctuation Chart

O	**period** - used at the end of a statement
?	**question mark**- used after a question
!	**exclamation mark**- used to show strong feelings
9	**comma** - used to pause or separate words
:	**colon** - used to start a list
;	**semi-colon** - used in place of the word "and"
" "	**quotation marks**- used to show when a character is speaking
( )	**parenthesis**- used to make a comment inside of a sentence

don't forget!

- Use capitals at the beginning of a sentence and for proper nouns.
- Use punctuation at the end of a sentence.
- Use quotations when someone is speaking.
- Highlight words you did not know how to spell.

Planning My Story

BEGINNING

MIDDLE

END

Words instead of "said"

Asked	Whispered	Explained	Sighed
Told	Shouted	Mumbled	Begged
Cried	Laughed	Yelled	Cheered
Wished	Squealed	Replied	Hugged

Name:_____

Word List

Treehouse
Adventure
Friend
Climb
Hideout
Fun

Title: _____

_____

- -

_____

- -

_____

- -

_____

_____

- -

_____

_____

- -

_____

- -

Name:_____

Word List

Museum
Dinosaur
Exhibit
Fossils
Prehistoric
Extinct

Title: _____

_____

_____

_____

_____

_____

_____

_____

_____

_____

_____

_____

_____

_____

_____

Name:_____

Word List

Horse
Lasso
Cowboy
Boots
Hat
Riding

Title:
_____
- -
_____
- -
_____
- -
_____
- -
_____
- -
_____
- -
_____
- -
_____

Name:_____

Word List

Forest
Hiking
Trees
Examine
Back Pack
Discover

Title:

_____
- -
_____
_____
- -
_____
_____
- -
_____
_____
- -
_____
_____
- -
_____
_____
- -
_____

Name:_____

Word List

Trash
Recycle
Clean
Tree
Yard
Earth

Title:_____

- -

_____

_____

- -

_____

_____

- -

_____

_____

- -

_____

_____

- -

_____

Word List

Scientist
Measure
Experiment
Mix
Beaker
Laboratory

Title:_____

Name:_____

Word List

Boat
Ocean
Shark
Sailors
Clouds
Surprise

Title:_____

_____

- -

_____

- -

_____

- -

_____

- -

_____

- -

_____

- -

_____

- -

Word List

Alien
Space
Planet
Rocket
Astronaut
Stars

Title: _____

- -
_____
- -
_____
- -
_____
- -
_____
- -
_____
- -
_____

Name:_____

Word List

Beach
Watermelon
Summer
Sandcastle
Umbrella
Ocean

Title: _____

_____
_____
_____
_____
_____
_____
_____
_____
_____
_____
_____
_____
_____
_____

Word List

Shark

Sea

Star Fish

Sand

Teeth

Fins

Title: _____

Word List

Mouse
Guitar
Drums
Music
Sing
Stage

Title: _____

_____

_____

_____

_____

_____

_____

_____

_____

Name:_____

Word List

Party
Balloons
Present
Tree
Friends
Hats

Title: _____

_____

_____

_____

_____

_____

_____

_____

_____

_____

_____

_____

_____

_____

_____

Picture Prompts Story Starters

Name:_____

Word List

**Plants
Cow
Farmer
Water
Plants
Grow**

Title:

Name:_____

Word List

Mermaid
Fish
Swim
Ocean
Turtle
Friends

Title: _____

_____
- -
_____
_____
- -
_____
_____
- -
_____
_____
- -
_____
_____
- -
_____
_____
- -
_____

Name:_____

Word List

Llama
Fishing
Candy
Heart
Ice Cream
Pond

Title: _____

Name:_____

Word List

Goggles
Snow
Mountains
Ski
Trees
Fast

Title:_____

- -
_____
_____
- -
_____
_____
- -
_____
_____
- -
_____
_____
- -
_____

Picture Prompts Story Starters   Name:_____

SPIKE

Word List

Giraffe
House
Tools
Kitten
Help
Friend

Title:
_____
- -
_____
_____
- -
_____
_____
- -
_____
_____
- -
_____
_____
- -
_____

Name:_____

Word List

Park
Kite
Wheelchair
Fun
Trees
Wind

Title: _____

- -
_____
- -
_____
- -
_____
- -
_____
- -
_____
- -
_____

Name:_____

Word List

Builder
Truck
Construction
Safety
Tools
Equipment

Title: _____

- -

_____

- -

_____

- -

_____

- -

_____

- -

_____

- -

_____

Word List

Pirate
Treasure
Parrot
Boat
Island
Ocean

Title: _____

- -
_____
- -
_____
- -
_____
- -
_____
- -
_____
- -
_____
- -
_____

Word List

Swimming
Water
Dog
Pet
Goggles
Fun

Title:

_____
- -
_____
- -
_____
- -
_____
_____
- -
_____
_____
- -
_____

Name:_____

Word List

Go Kart
Racing
Fast
Race Track
Drivers
Tires

Title:_____

_____
- - - - - - - - - - - - - - - - -
_____
_____
- - - - - - - - - - - - - - - - -
_____
_____
- - - - - - - - - - - - - - - - -
_____
_____
- - - - - - - - - - - - - - - - -
_____
_____
- - - - - - - - - - - - - - - - -
_____
_____
- - - - - - - - - - - - - - - - -
_____

Word List

Father
Son
Fishing
Boat
Fish
Lake

Title:
_____
- -
_____
- -
_____
- -
_____
_____
- -
_____
_____
- -
_____
_____
- -
_____

Word List

Bear
Family
Vacation
Bison
Park
Binoculars

Title: _____

_____

_____

_____

_____

_____

_____

_____

Name:_____

Word List

Classroom
Lion
Paper Plane
Window
Flying
Fast

Title:

_____

- -

_____

_____

- -

_____

_____

- -

_____

_____

- -

_____

_____

- -

_____

Name:_____

Word List

Beach
Trash
Clean Up
Lighthouse
Trees
Ocean

Title: _____

_____
- -
_____
_____
- -
_____
_____
- -
_____
_____
- -
_____
_____
- -
_____
_____
- -
_____

Name:_____

Word List

Camping
Tent
Forest
Guitar
Singing
Happy

Title:_____

_____
_____
_____
_____
_____
_____
_____
_____
_____
_____
_____
_____
_____
_____

Word List

Gorilla
Motorcycle
City
Street
Ride
Helmet

Title:
_____
- -
_____
_____
- -
_____
_____
- -
_____
_____
- -
_____
_____
- -
_____
_____
- -
_____

Word List

Winter
Snow
Sleigh
Bird
Hat
Scarf

Title: _____

- -
_____
- -
_____
- -
_____
- -
_____
- -
_____
- -
_____
- -
_____

Picture Prompts Story Starters   Name:_____

Word List

Octopus
Basketball
Goal
Player
Game
Score

Title:_____

_____
- -
_____
_____
- -
_____
_____
- -
_____
_____
- -
_____
_____
- -
_____
_____
- -
_____

Name:_____

Word List

Raft
River
Paddles
Helmet
Mountains
Fast

Title: _____

_____

_____

_____

_____

_____

_____

_____

_____

_____

_____

_____

_____

Name:_____

Word List

Koala Bear
Beach
Towel
Umbrella
Drink
Sand Pail

Title:_____

Word List

Alien
Pineapple
Planet
Stars
Explore
Galaxy

Title: _____

_____

_____

_____

_____

_____

_____

Name:_____

Word List

Monster
Happy
Clouds
Stars
Floating
Adventure

Title: _____

_____
- -
_____
_____
- -
_____
_____
- -
_____
_____
- -
_____
_____
- -
_____

Name:_____

Word List

Dinosaur

Happy

Bird

Volcanos

Lava

Mountain

Title:_____

_____

_____

_____

_____

_____

_____

_____

_____

_____

_____

_____

_____

_____

Name:_____

Word List

Race
Cars
Track
Fast
Team
Winner

Title:_____

Word List

Train
Ferris Wheel
Carnival
Kids
Waving
Happy

Title: _____

_____

_____

_____

_____

_____

_____

Name:_____

Word List

Skate Board
Helmet
Ramp
Flying
Fast
Park

Title: _____

_____
_____
_____
_____
_____
_____
_____
_____
_____
_____
_____
_____
_____
_____

Name:_____

Word List

Picnic
Friends
Happy
Park
Trees
Flowers

Title: _____

_____

_____

_____

_____

_____

_____

_____

_____

_____

_____

_____

_____

_____

_____

Picture Prompts Story Starters   Name:_____

Word List

Earth
Rocket
Planets
Stars
Space
Galaxy

Title:

_____

_____

_____

_____

_____

_____

Name:_____

Word List

Detective
Clue
Search
Mystery
Puzzle
Notes

Title: _____

_____

_____

_____

_____

_____

_____

_____

_____

_____

Name:_____

Word List

Basketball
Player
Goal
Score
Flying
Ice Cream

Title:
_____
- -
_____
- -
_____
_____
- -
_____
_____
- -
_____
_____
- -
_____
_____
- -
_____

Name:_____

Word List

Aquarium
Mermaid
Sharks
Mom
Brother
Sister

Title:
_____
- -
_____
- -
_____
- -
_____
- -
_____
- -
_____
- -
_____

Name:_____

Word List

Zebra
Stripes
Africa
Safari
Trees
Grass

Title:_____

Word List

Peacock
Teacher
Meerkat
Classroom
Desk
Homework

Title: _____

Name:_____

Word List

Fairies
Friends
Flying
Trees
Garden
Flowers

Title: _____

_____

_____

_____

_____

_____

_____

_____

_____

_____

_____

_____

_____

_____

Name:_____

Word List

Tractor
Dump Truck
City
Buildings
Help
Construction

Title: _____

- -
_____
- -
_____
- -
_____
- -
_____
- -
_____
- -
_____
- -
_____

Name:_____

Word List

Shoe
House
Lady Bug
Dragonfly
Forest
Leaves

Title: _____

Word List

Bear

Snake

Gecko

Skunk

Friends

Forest

Title: _____

- -
_____

_____
- -
_____

_____
- -
_____

_____
- -
_____

_____
- -
_____

Word List

Play
Share
Home
Train
Ball
Hats

Title: _____

- -

_____

_____

- -

_____

- -

_____

_____

- -

_____

_____

- -

_____

_____

- -

_____

Word List

Sea
Dolphin
Help
Fish
Octopus
Flowers

Title: _____

- -
_____
_____
- -
_____
_____
- -
_____
_____
- -
_____
_____
- -
_____
_____
- -
_____

Name:_____

Word List

Father
Son
Donate
Share
Food
Help

Title: _____

_____

- -

_____

- -

_____

- -

_____

- -

_____

- -

_____

- -

_____

- -

_____

Word List

Mermaid
Dolphin
Sea
Starfish
Clams
Friends

Title: _____

- -
_____
- -
_____
- -
_____
- -
_____
- -
_____
- -
_____
- -
_____

Word List

Boy
Superhero
Running
Fast
Dog
Best Friends

Title: _____

_____

_____

_____

_____

_____

_____

_____

_____

_____

_____

_____

_____

_____

_____

Name:_____

Word List

Umbrella

Ocean

Beach

Sandcastle

Pail

Shovel

Title: _____

_____

_____

_____

_____

_____

_____

_____

_____

_____

_____

_____

_____

_____

Word List

Boy
Crutches
Build
Rocket
Earth
Space

Title:_____

Name:_____

Word List

Wind
Fast
Robot
Science
Space
Planets

Title:
_____
- -
_____
- -
_____
_____
- -
_____
- -
_____
_____
- -
_____
- -
_____

Name:_____

Word List

Careful
Mountain
Climb
Helmet
Rope
Explore

Title: _____

_____

_____

_____

_____

_____

_____

Title: _____

_____

_____

_____

_____

_____

_____

_____

_____

_____

_____

_____

_____

_____

_____

_____

_____

_____

www.ingramcontent.com/pod-product-compliance
Lightning Source LLC
Chambersburg PA
CBHW081542040426
42448CB00015B/3184